A TEACHER'S GUIDE TO ORGANIZATIONAL STRATEGIES FOR THINKING AND WRITING

WRINKLES IN TEACHING:
A SERIES OF GUIDEBOOKS FOR TEACHERS

A *wrinkle* is "a useful piece of information," and one dictionary illustrates that by saying, "Learning the *wrinkles* from someone more experienced saves time." In the case of teaching, it also promotes faster, more effective student learning, it prevents unnecessary and frustrating bouts of trial and error, and it results in greater satisfaction with one's work. The "someone more experienced" is Billie Birnie, who taught successfully in elementary, middle, and senior high schools and then went on to observe and teach hundreds of teachers and, eventually, to write about her observations and experiences. Her books, designed for both elementary and secondary teachers, are short, practical, and down-to-earth conversations about the craft of teaching. *Organizational Strategies for Thinking and Writing* is the third in the series. The first was *Successful Classroom Management and Differentiated Instruction*, also by Dr. Birnie, and the second was *Practical Parenting and Learning Disabilities* by Susan Maynard. Other topics to come:

- Cooperative Learning
- Critical Thinking
- Assessing Writing Skill

Readers are welcome to suggest additional topics for the series. Suggestions should be sent to Rowman & Littlefield.

A TEACHER'S GUIDE TO ORGANIZATIONAL STRATEGIES FOR THINKING AND WRITING

Billie F. Birnie

ROWMAN & LITTLEFIELD
Lanham • Boulder • New York • London

Published by Rowman & Littlefield
A wholly owned subsidiary of The Rowman & Littlefield Publishing Group, Inc.
4501 Forbes Boulevard, Suite 200, Lanham, Maryland 20706
www.rowman.com

Unit A, Whitacre Mews, 26-34 Stannary Street, London SE11 4AB

British Library Cataloguing in Publication Information Available

Library of Congress Cataloging-in-Publication Data Available

ISBN 978-1-4758-1404-0 (pbk. : alk. paper)
ISBN 978-1-4758-1405-7 (electronic)

∞™ The paper used in this publication meets the minimum requirements
of American National Standard for Information Sciences—Permanence of
Paper for Printed Library Materials, ANSI/NISO Z39.48-1992.

Printed in the United States of America

CONTENTS

CONTENTS

PREFACE

Fran Claggett demonstrated the concept of "modeling" in one of the early years of the Glazer-Lorton Writing Institute in Miami, Florida. The term *modeling* in this context means imitating the style of another author by substituting your own words but retaining either the same parts of speech (*close modeling*) or the same overall structure (*loose* or *near modeling*). Having already experimented with this process as a teacher of English as a Second Language (we called it "pattern practice" then), I was once more impressed with its power for broadening one's repertoire of writing skills. I began to collect and compose passages that illustrated various ways to organize and express ideas—passages that could be used as models, or mentor texts, of those strategies. I was motivated not only by the prospect of sharpening my own thinking and writing skills but also by a desire to counteract the climate in many schools that promotes only one formula for writing.

The first time I used the models in a professional development session, one of the teachers asked where he could buy the book. I told him there was no book, just a small collection of examples. Since then, others have asked the same question. This book is a belated and, I trust, still welcome response.

Billie Birnie
Alpine, Texas
July 2014

ACKNOWLEDGMENTS

This book has been taking shape over many years, and its development has been nourished by a number of people. Chief among them are the following:

- Dr. Eveleen Lorton, mentor, friend, professor emerita of the University of Miami in Coral Gables, Florida, and co-founder of the Glazer-Lorton Writing Institute in Miami, Florida, for her constant support and inspiration;
- Fran Claggett, nationally recognized author and consultant, whose demonstration of modeling reawakened my interest in the process;
- Two groups of teachers who first tested the assignments in this book and who responded with enthusiasm and encouragement: elementary and secondary teachers who attended the Writing Institute, and English and social studies teachers in Monroe County, Florida;
- Sister Suzanne Cooke, former headmistress of Carrollton School of the Sacred Heart in Coconut Grove, Florida, and now Head of the Conference of Sacred Heart Education in the United States and Canada, who commissioned three series of seminars that focused on the strategies in this book;
- The seminar participants: Sister Margaret Seitz, assistant headmistress; Heather Gillingham-Rivas and Paola Consuegra, directors of the intermediate and primary schools, respectively; and teachers Shaune Scott, Rob Pollock, Patti Bruno, Margie Nunez-Ismael, Julia Cornett,

Lourdes Aguiar, Maritza Fernandez, Maria Bernal, Anna Cristina Cammarano, Christie Diaz, Cristina Fano, Lizette Gomez, Maggie Jones, Iris Kovacs, Jessica Lamp'l, Nina Obregon, Cristina Pelleya, Lissette Ruiz, Natalie Eskert, Brittney Hernandez, Maria Jones, Louris Otero, Anna Peraza, Briana Tateo, and Monica Viola;

- Colleagues who gave me permission to use their writing as models: Donna Tobey, Head of the Lower School, Palm Beach Day Academy; Jeanne Sanford, former coordinator of social studies, Monroe District Schools (now retired); and from Carrollton, Ms. Gillingham-Rivas, Ms. Fano, and Ms. Otero;
- The published authors whose work provided some of the models: Count Philippe Paul de Ségur (and the translator of his book, J. David Townsend), S. C. Gwynne, Barry Lopez, Fitzroy McLean, and David Mitchell;
- Fran Ginsberg, who allowed me to describe her use of response groups;
- Joanie Cobo, who read the manuscript and offered valuable suggestions; and
- Vice President and Editorial Director Tom Koerner, Associate Editor Carlie Wall, Assistant Editor Christine Fahey, and Production Editor Melissa McNitt of Rowman & Littlefield, who provided editorial assistance.

I am grateful to all of those people for their contributions to this effort.

Two colleagues whose untimely deaths robbed the educational community of their leadership also influenced my thinking: Zelda Glazer, cofounder of the writing institute that bears her name, and Norma Bossard, who succeeded Zelda as director of language arts in the Miami-Dade County Public Schools.

Finally, I wish to thank my husband, Richard, who has supported this work since its inception. He read the manuscript after every one of the numerous revisions and offered many insightful suggestions for its improvement.

Billie Birnie
Alpine, Texas
July 2014

INTRODUCTION

This book is for teachers of academic subjects that require written expression. It will help you take your students from wherever they are on the ladder of writing and thinking skills to mastery of the rigorous standards established for today's students. Just as teachers relatively recently realized that all teachers are teachers of reading, they are now beginning to recognize that they are also teachers of writing—because writing is the visual expression of thinking, and thinking is every teacher's domain.

The book contains three major sections: some *preliminaries* that will prepare you and your students for the process of modeling, instructions for *how to use the rest of the book*, and ten models of *organizational strategies*, each illustrated with at least two passages of mentor texts. The first six models are the basic patterns of organization: chronological, spatial, topical, comparison, contrast, and comparison-contrast. The last four are less well-known patterns that offer a variety of approaches to thinking and writing: question-answer, traditional narrative, point-counterpoint, and extended analogy.

Each of the ten patterns is illustrated by mentor texts appropriate for secondary students, college students, and adults. The first eight patterns also include two additional mentor texts, one for writers in the early grades and another for writers in the middle grades. Those examples will also be useful with students of any age who are just beginning to write or who are just learning English.

Following the description and examples is a summarizing table that names each of the strategies and tells what it does, when to introduce it, appropriate prewriting strategies, sample transitional words, and sample writing tasks that use the pattern.

The book concludes with a bonus: a lesson on modeling rhythm and rhyme in poetry.

It may be that some of your students who read widely and already write well would not benefit from the practice this book provides. If you have such students, they should be allowed to develop their writing and thinking skills without being required to follow specific patterns of organization.

PRELIMINARIES

This section offers some essential information that will pave the way for successful use of the strategies that follow. Whether you teach elementary or secondary students, you will want to use the writing process with them; ensure that they know the basics of sentences, paragraphs, and longer compositions; understand how modeling works; and know how to work with classmates in response groups.

THE WRITING PROCESS

The writing process involves several stages. They may or may not occur in the same order for every writing task. Rather than being linear, the process is recursive, with stages overlapping and often recurring. So, although each stage is described below in the order it usually occurs, writers should be aware that the order may change with the demands of the task at hand.

Prewriting. This stage involves thinking about the writing ahead, perhaps choosing or narrowing a topic; selecting a point of view, approach, or framework for presenting the subject; and even thinking about details, anecdotes, or images that will develop the subject. Activities that frequently occur during this stage are reading selections that contribute to the writer's grasp of the subject; viewing films, DVDs, or pictures that deal with the topic; jot-listing, clustering, or mapping ideas; and talking to other people about the ideas.

Planning. The planning stage, while still "prewriting" in the sense that it usually occurs before the actual writing, involves recording a plan for the finished piece. The plan may be as formal as an outline or as informal as a list, a diagram, or a map to guide the writing.

Drafting. In the drafting stage, the writer creates a flow of thought, connecting ideas into phrases or sentences on paper and perhaps, if the plan works, moving directly to paragraphs or even chapters. The writer is not preoccupied with correctness at this point; it is more important to get the ideas down on paper than to maintain adherence to the plan or to be concerned with mechanical aspects of writing such as spelling, punctuation, or capitalization.

The purpose of this stage is to put words on paper, to create text. Until the text exists, there is no "writing," no matter how much you have thought about your topic. The result of drafting may be simply a free flow of ideas or it may be a fairly coherent draft.

Revising. By revising, the writer makes the piece better. Depending on the condition of the draft, this stage may require anything from Band-Aids (refining word choice, amplifying a detail or two, or combining sentences) to major surgery (reordering chunks of writing, filling gaps left by the drafting, or deleting whole sections). In this stage, the writer asks, "Does this passage convey the intended meaning?" Reading the piece aloud, asking for responses from others, or leaving the passage alone for a time and then seeing it afresh are techniques that aid revision.

Editing. By editing, the author (or editor) makes the writing mechanically correct. In this stage, attention turns to the details of variety in sentence length and structure and the conventions of language: spelling, punctuation, capitalization, and standard usage.

Sharing. In this stage, the writing reaches its intended audience. If the composition fulfills its purpose, this stage concludes the process. However, as pointed out earlier, sharing is not only the final stage; it may be useful as well when the author is prewriting, planning, and revising.

All of that being said, the writer (and the teacher of writing) must remember that writing is a highly individualized process that manifests thinking and that not only is it different for every person, it may change with every writing task for the same author.

WHAT STUDENTS MUST KNOW ABOUT SENTENCES

Every sentence requires five things: (1) a capital letter at the beginning, (2) a punctuation mark at the end, (3) a subject, (4) a predicate, and (5) a complete thought. The three punctuation marks that can be used to end sentences are a period (.), a question mark (?), and an exclamation point (!). The *subject* is who or what the sentence is about. The *predicate* tells what the subject is or does.

If you have not written a sentence, you have written either a *fragment* or a *run-on*.

A fragment is a group of words that does not make a complete thought. A fragment may be corrected by one of two ways: (1) add words or (2) subtract words.

A run-on is two or more complete thoughts, punctuated incorrectly as one sentence. A run-on may be corrected by one of four ways: (1) Separate the thoughts with a period. (Remember to start the new sentence with a capital letter.) (2) Separate the thoughts with a semi-colon (;). (3) Connect the thoughts with a comma and a coordinating conjunction (e.g., *and, but, or, nor, for, yet*). (4) Subordinate one of the thoughts with a subordinating conjunction (e.g., *when, if, because, although, since, unless*).

Extensive reading of good literature imbues the reader with an understanding of these structural characteristics so that they are automatically incorporated into written expression. Students clearly need guidance in selecting good literature from someone who understands the difference between good and mediocre prose.

Teachers should also recognize that effective writing often breaks traditional rules. Consider, for instance, Virginia Tufte's enlightening book, *Artful Sentences: Syntax as Style*, which offers hundreds of examples of effective sentences, many of which defy convention. While the basic rules of sentence structure can provide a foundation for beginning writers, they should not become a straitjacket.

WHAT STUDENTS MUST KNOW ABOUT PARAGRAPHS

The traditionally structured paragraph involves six components. The *topic sentence*, frequently the first in the paragraph, tells both what the paragraph will be about and what the author will say about that subject. It is followed by *supporting details* that elaborate on the subject. Details may be facts, incidents, reasons, examples, statistics (often taught with the use of the acronym FIRES), or a combination of those.

In a longer paragraph, details are often linked by *transitional devices*, words or phrases that help the reader shift from one idea to the next. Transitional devices may be the repetition of key words, the use of pronouns that refer to key words, or linking words or phrases such as *however*, *although*, or *next*. Details are presented in some kind of logical arrangement, such as time, place, or importance, to give the paragraph *coherence*, or logical order (or, as Patrick O'Brian says in *Treason's Harbour*, "flow, cohesion, natural sequence" [p. 235]).

It is important that all of the sentences in the paragraph develop only what is predicted in the topic sentence, staying within appropriate boundaries and thus establishing *unity*, or a sense of oneness. A traditionally structured paragraph often ends with a *clincher sentence* that summarizes the details, restates the main idea, or simply concludes the paragraph satisfactorily. The use of all six components will ensure a well-organized paragraph; it is up to the writer, then, to be sure that what is said is significant and interesting.

WHAT STUDENTS MUST KNOW ABOUT ESSAYS

The traditionally structured essay, often called the "chain paragraph essay," is simply an expanded version of the traditionally structured paragraph. The first paragraph, or *introduction*, which includes the thesis statement, or controlling idea, is analogous to the paragraph's topic sentence. Succeeding paragraphs form the *body* of the composition, just as the details form the middle of the paragraph. The *conclusion*, or last paragraph of the essay, acts the same way the clincher sentence does for the paragraph, providing a satisfactory ending to the composition.

Paragraphs are arranged logically, in the order predicted in the introduction, to achieve *coherence*: They are linked appropriately through *transitional devices*; and they fulfill the "promise" of the thesis statement, achieving *unity*.

Mastery of the traditionally structured essay, coupled with abundant knowledge of the subject, has contributed to academic success for countless students. This format serves well on timed assessments, standardized tests that require essays, and in high school and college classes that require compositions. However, the structure of the essay alone cannot compensate for a lack of knowledge about the topic; good writing demands both substance and structure.

Organizational Strategies. Organizational strategies are different ways of developing ideas effectively through language (either spoken or written). Some of the most common are comparison, contrast, definition, emphasis (order of importance), analysis of process, and logical reasoning. Other strategies are question-answer, point-counterpoint, extended analogy, and traditional narrative. The serious student continually works to build a repertoire of strategies. (Kelly Gallagher offers these additional strategies in his book *Write Like This: Teaching Real-World Writing Through Modeling and Mentor Texts*: Express and Reflect, Inform and Explain, Evaluate and Judge, Inquire and Explore, Analyze and Interpret, Take a Stand/Propose a Solution.)

Tone. In writing, *tone*, or attitude, is the author's attitude toward the subject. The more adept an author is at making that attitude clear, the more tone contributes to the success of the composition and the clearer the "persona," or voice, of the writer. Tone has almost infinite variations, from humorous to neutral to sober, from friendly to objective to scathing, from informal to sophisticated. As with organizational strategies, the more attitudes an author can adeptly assume, the more choices for successfully conveying meaning to a reader.

Style. Style is the way in which the author uses language. A journalistic style, such as that used by Ernest Hemingway, is straightforward and economical. A more elaborate style, chosen by authors such as William Faulkner, uses long sentences, abundant description, and oblique approaches. Young writers will want to examine different styles used by professional writers and also experiment with different styles for different purposes.

Range of Vocabulary. A writer's *range of vocabulary* is determined both by the number of words available for use and the precision with which those words are employed. Again, as with organizational strategies and attitudes, the wider the range, the better the writing will be. A writer with a narrow range reuses a small number of words and finds difficulty in being precise or sometimes uses words incorrectly; a writer with a wide range adds precision, imagination, figurative language (such as metaphor, simile, personification), freshness, and depth to the composition.

HOW MODELING WORKS

Modeling is one of the most effective paths to improving writing skill. It enables the novice to write sentences, the more advanced student to write paragraphs, and even the most able writers to broaden their range of skills.

Two kinds of modeling are available: (a) close and (b) near, or loose. (Fran Claggett discusses both at length in chapter IX of her book *Teaching Writing: Craft, Art, Genre.*) Close modeling demands that the writer reproduce exact grammatical structures, using the same number of words in the new sentence as in the model. For instance, if the pattern sentence is "Birds fly," the new sentence might be "Flowers bloom" or "Dogs bark." The pattern, in this case, requires a plural subject, an active verb, and a simple subject-predicate sentence.

Near modeling, on the other hand, allows the writer more latitude: A near model of the same sentence could be any simple subject-predicate structure, such as "My mother cooked" or "The sun is shining."

The exercises in this book ask for near modeling. Their purpose is not to constrain the writer by demanding exact fidelity to every word, but rather to expose the student to patterns of organization. Neither the grammatical structure nor the number of words is prescribed. On the contrary, for each strategy, at least two examples are offered, and those examples often vary in length and structure.

THE USE OF RESPONSE GROUPS

One approach to teaching writing in a traditional classroom setting is the use of response groups. If you wish to use that approach, these guidelines may be helpful.

- If possible, the group should be from three to five in number, and it should be stable throughout the completion of the exercises. As students work together on their writing, trust develops, responses become more helpful, and improvement gathers momentum.
- If there is a wide range of writing skill in your class, the group should contain members of different skill levels.
- Everyone in the group must participate in every meeting.
- The piece of writing under consideration should be read aloud to the group, preferably by the author.
- The author is encouraged to ask for suggestions about aspects of the writing that are especially challenging.
- Members of the group are encouraged to ask the author clarifying questions about the writing.

- Members should praise specific aspects of the writing that are especially well done.
- Suggestions to improve the writing are just that; it is the author's prerogative to use them or not. (The author always "owns" the writing.)
- If the assignment or the teacher gives directions for specific activities such as TAG (**t**ell something you like, **a**sk a question, **g**ive a suggestion), the group should follow those directions.
- If a meeting is scheduled for hearing more than one piece of writing, time should be carefully allocated so that everyone's writing receives the same amount of time.

Fran Ginsberg, an accomplished teacher of both middle school and high school English language arts, made effective use of response groups in her classes. At the beginning of the year, after assessing students' writing skill, she divided each class into triads. In each group were a relatively skilled writer, a moderate performer, and a relatively unskilled writer. Then she drilled them on how to move quickly and quietly into position: three desks, side by side and as close together as possible, separated from the other triads by as much as space allowed.

After each writing assignment was drafted, students moved quickly and quietly into their groups. The student whose writing was under consideration sat in the middle desk, reading aloud while the other two students looked at the paper as well. This arrangement enabled the hearers to see what the author was reading, and it added considerably to the effectiveness of the work.

During the time allowed for the groups to discuss the assignment, the students rotated so that each of them sat in the middle chair for the same amount of time. Fran circulated during this activity, listening to the students, prompting engagement when necessary, and offering praise or suggestions as appropriate. For a long or an especially difficult assignment, the groups might meet two or three times before the finished papers were submitted for the teacher's assessment.

Remember that, in writing as in other subjects, one size does not fit all. Writing can be and often is a very personal endeavor. Some students may do better working on their own or asking for help from a trusted person who is not in the class—a parent, brother, sister, friend, another teacher, the librarian, or someone else. The teacher who honors students' preferences will enable all of them to thrive in learning environments suited to their needs.

HOW TO USE THE REST OF THIS BOOK

First and most important, practice the strategies before you ask your students to use them. If you are satisfied with your work, use it in addition to the models in this book, so that your students will know that you are not asking them to do something you cannot do yourself. In fact, that advice goes for any assignment you make: Do it yourself first, so that you thoroughly understand what you're asking students to do. Not only will you improve your own skill, you will also increase your credibility with your students. As Norma Bossard said, "A teacher who doesn't write can teach *about* writing, but she cannot teach writing."

One approach for familiarizing teachers with the strategies has been used successfully at Carrollton School of the Sacred Heart in Coconut Grove, Florida. Each year, a different group of teachers participates in a series of seminars that focus on the models. Teachers of all subjects, not just those who teach English, participate in the seminars. After carefully examining the mentor texts and discussing their structure, teachers write their own paragraphs using the strategy. After drafting on their own, they work either in formal response groups or in informal partnerships to review their writing. Then they polish, revise, and submit their paragraphs to the facilitator.

Finished pieces are read by the authors and critiqued in each seminar, either by the facilitator or other participants. A new strategy is then introduced for the next assignment. By the end of the year, teachers have a collection of their own paragraphs as well as access to those of their colleagues. In addition, they have a heightened appreciation of what it takes to produce good writing.

After reviewing the strategies, you may find that your students need only some of the models. If that is the case, select the ones they need and use those with your classes. The strategies also offer a ready means for differentiating instruction. If some of your students need all of the strategies and others only some, make assignments based on their individual needs.

The following guidelines are designed for the teacher who will be using the strategies with a class of students. If you are working with adults or on your own, they may not apply.

- Read the models and accompanying comments aloud in class. (Each model should be read in its entirety by one able reader, either the teacher or a student who has prepared for the reading. Another competent reader may read the comments that precede and follow the models.)
- Discuss the strategy. Bring to the discussion your own experience in using the strategy, telling about particular challenges and offering insights that you gained from completing the assignment. Be sure that all of the students understand the structure of the model before moving on. If you're not sure of their understanding, work through a sample draft with the large group, producing a paragraph that all of your students can see and copy. This analysis is essential; it lays the foundation for students to follow the model.
- Make the assignment. If, in addition to modeling the strategy, you want students to practice other writing skills, tell them now. For instance, you may want them to avoid using first person (*I, me, my, we, us, our*), or you may want them to select a topic related to the subject under study (e.g., a period of history, a novel, a science unit).
- Ask students to think of topics appropriate for that strategy. (You may want them to meet in small groups to talk about appropriate topics, or you may want to conduct a large-group discussion, listing possible topics for all to see.)
- Allow students time to select a topic (at least overnight—not within the same class period in which the strategy was introduced).
- Ask them to draft a paragraph of 100 to 300 words that models the strategy. (If you teach in the early grades, adjust the length accordingly.)
- If you are using response groups, allow the groups to review the drafts. If you want them to use a particular approach, such as mirroring (simply reflecting what they hear), tell them so.

- If you use one-on-one conferences, confer with individual students so that you can offer appropriate praise and suggestions.
- If you are using neither response groups nor one-on-one conferences, encourage students to find at least one other person who will listen to the paper and respond to it.

Allow students time to revise their drafts. You may want to suggest specific tasks for them that are appropriate for their age and level of development. Here are some suggestions you might make:

- See how many sensory details you included (words or phrases that evoke the senses of sight, touch, taste, smell, or hearing). Add more if they will improve your paper.
- Count the number of words in each sentence. Consider adding or subtracting words if necessary to add variety to sentence length.
- Read your sentences for structure. If they all begin with the subject and end with the predicate, consider changing the word order. If they are all simple sentences (only one independent clause with a subject and predicate), consider combining some sentences to make them compound (two or more independent clauses) or complex (one or more independent clauses, one or more dependent clauses). If you find a sentence that is so long that it "loses its way," break it up into shorter, clearer sentences.
- Look at every verb. Is it the best possible verb for that subject, or would another word be more active, more vivid, more precise?
- See if you have inadvertently repeated any words or ideas. If you have, use different words or delete the unnecessary repetition.
- Look for unintentional use of slang (e.g., *kids* instead of *children*, *cops* instead of *policemen*). If you find any, substitute standard words.

- Allow students time to edit their work. (Remember that editing is the process that makes the writing mechanically correct. This is the point at which students should be sure that verbs agree with their subjects, that pronouns agree with their antecedents, and that spelling, punctuation, and capitalization adhere to accepted conventions.) This is the point at which a handbook on grammar and usage can be helpful. One of the best for secondary and college students is Strunk and White's *Elements of Style.*

- Ask students to write a final draft and submit it for your judgment. Remind them of requirements for formatting if you have preferences.

THE STRATEGIES

CHRONOLOGICAL ORDER

Chronological order means arrangement of details in the order of time, or as they occurred. The following paragraph illustrates this by tracing a family from one generation to the next. It comes from S. C. Gwynne's book *Empire of the Summer Moon*:

> Ranald Slidell Mackenzie came from one of those prodigiously overachieving eastern seaboard families that seemed connected, in profound and unaccountable ways, to everyone who was anyone in the corridors of power. His grandfather John Slidell was a Manhattan bank president and political power broker in New York City. His uncle John Jr. became the most powerful man in Louisiana politics, a U.S. senator, and the top adviser to President James Buchanan. Mackenzie's aunt Jane married Commodore Matthew Perry, the man who opened Japan to the West. Aunt Julia married a rear admiral. Uncle Thomas became chief justice of Louisiana. His father, Alexander Mackenzie Slidell, who reversed his last and middle names at the request of a maternal uncle, was both a prominent naval commander and a well-known writer of histories and travel books who once had the distinction of being court-martialed for hanging the son of the secretary of war for mutiny. His mother came from splendid bloodlines, too: Her grandfather had been assistant secretary of the treasury under Alexander Hamilton." (p. 235)

(Mackenzie was the federal army officer who was responsible for the defeat of the Comanches.)

Following is another paragraph that uses chronological order. Its facts come from the same book, *Empire of the Summer Moon*.

The life of Quanah Parker shifted dramatically from the time of his father's death and his mother's abduction until his own death 50 years later. The last of the great Comanche chiefs, Quanah was only twelve when his Comanche father, Peter Nocona, was killed and his white mother, Cynthia Ann Parker, forcibly taken back to her relatives, leaving Quanah and his younger brother to fend for themselves. A trek on foot through more than a hundred miles of unpopulated high plains took the two youngsters to the main Comanche settlement. There they were allowed to stay, but they were treated harshly, as the orphans they were. Quanah, being strong and determined not to be a victim, proved himself as an aggressive young warrior. By his late teens, he was leading war parties, and by his twenties, he was widely recognized as a foremost chief of his people. When federal forces subdued the warring Comanches and confined the Indians to reservations, Quanah adapted quickly. He learned English, dressed in white man's clothes, built a large frame house to accommodate his growing family, and counseled his people to learn the ways of their former enemies. When he died at 62, Quanah had successfully transformed himself from a primitive Indian of the plains to a cultivated political leader in the white man's world.

Both paragraphs begin with a *topic sentence*, a general statement that tells what the paragraph is going to be about and what the author is going to say about the topic. They continue with *supporting details* that "fulfill the promise" of the topic sentence, and they conclude logically, the first without a *"clincher sentence"* and the second with one. The other elements of a traditionally structured paragraph are also present: *transitional devices* that link one idea to the next (in the first paragraph, the forebears' relationship to Mackenzie—grandfather, uncle, etc.; in the second, Quanah's age); *coherence* (the logical arrangement of ideas, provided in both cases by the order of time); and *unity* (focusing on one idea).

Models Appropriate for the Early Grades

It takes four steps to preview a book. First, look at the covers, front and back. Then read what other people said about the book. Next, read about the author. Fourth, look at the Table of Contents. Fifth, look at pictures if there are any. Now you're ready to begin reading.

Each season has something special. Spring brings nice days and flowers. Summer means we can go to the beach on hot days. In the fall we get to go back to school, and the leaves turn red. Winter has snowmen and hot chocolate.

Model Appropriate for the Middle Grades

One effective way to study a textbook assignment is PQRST. First, *preview* the chapter. Check to see how long it is. Look at headlines and any pictures, graphs, or tables, reading the captions below them. Second, using your preview as a guide, ask *questions* that you think the chapter might answer. Write the questions down. Next, *read* the chapter. Then close the book and *summarize* the chapter in your own words. Finally, *test* yourself to see if you can answer the questions you asked. This process will enable you to understand the material and enhance your learning.

SPATIAL ORGANIZATION

Spatial, or geographic, organization allows the writer to discuss a subject in terms of space, or place. Here is one example.

Some people say that books will give way to electronic text, but that will never happen in this home. Books are shelved, stacked, laid, and marked in every room of the house. In the kitchen are the cookbooks used last night, still open on the cabinet top, stars and notations vying with the lists of ingredients and beautiful photographs of Jacques Pepin's dishes. In the dining room, more cookbooks line the shelves, along with newly purchased finds from local book stores that haven't even been read yet: Tananarive Due's novel *The Between*, the autobiographical tale of Tamara McIntyre's childhood in China, a scientific treatise on the Gulf Stream. Between the dining and living room is a credenza, where *Let Me Hear Your Voice* lies waiting for a reader's return, bookmark in place, and Rudyard Kipling's *The Man Who Would Be King* invites a second look. By a chair in the living room rests *The Death of Common Sense*, and on the shelves against the wall, dozens of family treasures: first editions of Macaulay's essays, anthologies of favorite poems, biographies of earlier generations, leather-bound gems and yellow-paged friends. The den, the loft, the bedroom are packed with books as well. On shelves, in baskets, on tables, on the floor, books read, books waiting to be read, books ready for a third, or fifth, or seventh reading. Electronic text may someday be included, but it will never replace the real thing in this household.

In the example above, the passage opens with a statement about the topic, followed immediately by the prediction of the organization: "Books . . . in every room of the house." The idea is developed as the writer "keeps the promise" of the thesis by describing the books in each room of the home. It ends with a strong clincher that sums up the main idea of the paragraph and brings it full circle, back to the idea expressed in the opening sentence.

Following is a passage that uses the same pattern: opening sentence to introduce the topic, second sentence to predict the spatial organization, several sentences to fulfill the prediction, and clincher sentence that returns to the main idea.

Idyllic anchorages abound in the near-shore waters of South Florida. Cruising south from Miami, the boater is blessed with choices for all weather. If it's blowing hard, the captain will want to tuck into the first good spot south of the city, Boca Chita Basin, protected on all sides and guarded by the towering, picturesque lighthouse. The basin offers docks, rock bridges over winding inland waterways, palm and pine trees, and inviting picnic sites. If the wind is from the east or south, a half-mile further takes cruisers to the anchorage off Sands Key, spacious yet still protected. A short dinghy ride will carry them from the anchorage into the almost landlocked "keyhole" of water surrounded by mangroves and wading birds. East wind blowing? Elliott Key offers miles of protected anchorages, from Lewis Cut at the north end to Billy's Point and Caesar Creek at the south. Crystalline waters over white sand offer an open invitation for swimming and snorkeling along this stretch of Biscayne Bay, and boaters who go ashore may explore the whole length and breadth of the island, from the Atlantic shore on the east to the bay shore on the west. For a longer day of cruising and a perfect anchorage in any weather, the best destination is Pumpkin Key, a fat pancake of tree-covered land in Card Sound, south of Biscayne Bay. By the time the sailors arrive at

Pumpkin Key, they can hear the siren songs of both the Florida Keys and the Bahamas, for channels to both are within sight. No wonder South Florida is known as a boater's paradise.

Spatial organization works well for memoir, too, as Louris Otero demonstrates in this poignant remembrance of her childhood neighborhood:

When I stand at the edge of the sidewalk, I can almost hear the kids playing. Looking down its length, I can clearly remember specific spots teeming with memories. This is where, as Shel Silverstein put it, my sidewalk ends. This is the street I grew up on. My childhood home, one of only a handful of houses on the whole block, sits at the intersection of Southwest 23rd Street and 70th Avenue in Westchester. Across the street and next door on the left are apartment buildings where I spent countless hours swimming, running, and hiding. On the right are the other two houses, where my long-time neighbors lived and raised their families. From the sidewalk, you can see up and down the street to the railroad tracks that flank my block on both ends. If you take a walk along the sidewalk, you can see the metal grate that made that familiar clanging sound when we rode over it with our bikes and skates. Across the street is the exact spot where I stood, paralyzed in my Roller Derby skates with the black pompoms, the day the ambulance came because my friend cut her arm on a piece of glass. Walk on a little further and you will come across the telephone pole: a sentry, standing straight and smelling of Creolin, where we hid our eyes and counted while playing *Hide-and-Go-Seek*. The telephone pole also served as the imaginary boundary, the limit of my outside playground. Look up and you can see the spot on the second floor hallway where my piano-playing friend, Jose, stood as I yelled at him to get his bike and come downstairs. That was the day I taught him to ride a bike because I wanted him to pull me while I skated. Oh! Wait! Did you hear that? My mom just whistled for me. *I gotta go*! See you tomorrow!

Model Appropriate for the Early Grades

Our classroom is perfect. The ceiling has bright lights that help us see. The north wall has a chalkboard and a door. The west wall is full of windows. The south wall has bulletin boards. The east wall has bookcases. In the middle are our desks. In the southeast corner is our library.

Model Appropriate for the Middle Grades

The state of Texas has five different areas. In the north is the Panhandle, between Oklahoma on the east and New Mexico on the west. Just below the Panhandle and extending westward to El Paso is West Texas. Just east of West Texas is Central Texas, the middle of the state. To the east is East Texas, which borders Louisiana. Finally, there is South Texas, between the Gulf of Mexico on the east and Mexico on the west.

TOPICAL ORGANIZATION

Topical organization divides a whole into its component parts and deals with the parts in a logical order. The following paragraph on the beliefs of teachers illustrates the technique.

The complex craft of teaching encompasses numerous skills and qualities, combined in a different way in every teacher. The best of teachers, however, share some common beliefs. They believe that all children can learn. When they face a group of children with a wide range of talent, they recognize that, while the pace and degree of learning are different for every child, every child can and will learn in their classroom. Good teachers also know that teaching is important. Indeed, many view their career as a calling rather than a job, and the zeal with which they meet the challenges of each day attests to that abiding sense of mission. Far from being too serious, though, effective teachers also know that teaching and learning are fun. They laugh with their children. They share the joy of discovery—and they help their children enjoy themselves as well. Finally, the best teachers recognize that whether or not their students learn, what they learn, and how successfully they learn may well depend more on the teacher than on the students, especially in the beginning. In essence, they tell their children, "If you fail, I fail; and I don't intend to fail." These four beliefs sustain the work of good teachers everywhere. They are the foundation for success in thousands of classrooms.

Notice that, contrary to the most common pattern of organization, the first sentence is not the topic sentence. It leads to the topic sentence, which is the second sentence. The "whole" in this case is "common beliefs." The "parts" are the individual beliefs—all children can learn, teaching is important, teaching and learning are fun, and initial responsibility for learning is the teacher's.

Following is another example of a paragraph that uses topical organization. This one follows the same pattern: an introductory sentence that "leads in" to the topic sentence; the topic sentence; and the supporting details, which are subtopics of the "whole."

Helping students improve their writing is a major goal for most teachers of academic subjects. To achieve that goal, teachers must do four things. First, they must immerse their students in literacy, bathing them in words and surrounding them with reading and writing. Such immersion includes the teachers' own involvement with literacy, manifest by reading aloud to students, sharing their own writing, and "thinking aloud" about the value of the written word. Second, they must ask students to write frequently and follow up with responses to the writing that include praise for aspects of the writing that are well done and corrective suggestions about aspects of the writing that can be improved. (Research reports that frequency of writing alone does not improve students' writing; only when it is accompanied by specific praise and judicious counsel for improvement does the quality improve.) Third, teachers must provide direct instruction in how to write. They must teach their students the process of writing, the requirements of various kinds of compositions, the types of organization, a variety of rhetorical strategies, and the conventions of writing. Finally, they must read themselves and encourage their students to read—not just anything, but good literature. If they do these four things consistently, their students will undoubtedly become able writers.

Following is another paragraph that uses topical organization. Unlike the first two examples, this one begins with a straightforward topical sentence. Cristina Fano describes the conditions that produce a hardwood hammock:

The hardwood hammock is a natural habitat found in South Florida. Due to the unique conditions of the hardwood hammock, a forest of tropical plants and trees is able to thrive in this environment. Tropical hardwood hammocks are slightly elevated, allowing them to remain dry even during the rainy season. The shallow roots of hardwood trees such as the Gumbo Limbo, Cocoplum, and Mahogany find water in the cracks of the limestone rock beneath the forest floor. Solution holes form as the acidic mixture of decaying organic material and rain erodes the limestone, creating pits that fill with water. These solution holes keep the habitat humid and moist. Natural shade occurs as the hardwood trees grow close together, creating a thick canopy of intersecting branches that shade the densely vegetated understory. The occurrence of the tropical hardwood hammock relies on this rare and unusual setting found only in the Florida Everglades.

Model Appropriate for the Early Grades

A flower has four main parts. The base of the flower is the sepal. It is usually green. The petals are the prettiest part. They can be lots of different colors. Inside the petals are the stamen and the pistil, the parts that attract bees and hummingbirds.

Model Appropriate for the Middle Grades

Arithmetic can be divided into four functions. The simplest is addition, through which numbers are combined, such as in 1 plus 1 equals 2. Subtraction is the opposite of addition. When one number is subtracted from another, it is taken away. For instance, 5 minus 3 equals 2. Multiplication uses the times tables to arrive at combinations of numbers, such as 2 times 2 equals 4. The most complicated function is division, by which numbers are separated into parts. For example, 10 divided by 2 equals 5. These four functions form the foundation of mathematics.

COMPARISON

When people compare two or more subjects, they may look at both similarities and differences. However, this strategy looks only at similarities. A passage developed in this manner focuses on ways in which the subjects are alike. It does not treat differences. Here is an example:

Vertie Flack is like the Walker women of Texas. She isn't actually a member of the Walker family, but somewhere along the line she picked up the same traits they have. Her sense of humor is the same; she sees humor in almost everything, especially the little chuckle-producing incidents that pop up in daily life. She's independent, too, as the Walkers are. Not the beaten path for Vertie; she'll blaze her own trail, thank you. And that drive to be sure her work is just right, leaving no detail undone, no loose ends hanging, is the same drive that characterizes three generations of Walker women. Vertie's enough like them that she could attend a family reunion and be right at home.

In the example above, the first sentence introduces the two topics to be compared: Vertie Flack and the Walker women. Then the passage cites three similarities: sense of humor, independence, and follow-through. It concludes by "tying up the package" with a clincher sentence. Following is another passage that follows the same pattern:

Civilization emerged about 3,000 B.C. in the Middle Eastern countries of Egypt and Mesopotamia, countries that shared three important similarities. First were the rivers, the Nile in Egypt and the Tigris and Euphrates in Mesopotamia; their water nourished arable lands that produced crops to feed large populations. Second was autocratic rule, dominated by a succession of pharaohs in Egypt and kings in Mesopotamia; it curtailed individual freedom, but it ensured survival and order. Third was the desire to dominate their neighbors; both countries conquered adjacent communities, paving the way for their emergence as history's first great empires. Although the two birthplaces of civilization developed independently, they had much in common.

Model Appropriate for the Early Grades

"Cinderella" and "Snow White" have three things that are alike. Both stories are about beautiful girls. Both have mean women, the stepmother and the witch. They both have handsome princes that rescue the girls. That's why I like them.

Model Appropriate for the Middle Grades

George Washington and Abraham Lincoln were alike in three ways. Both of them were important men during wars. George Washington was the hero of the American Revolution, and Abraham Lincoln led the country through the Civil War. Both men stood for right. Washington helped win independence from England, and Lincoln helped abolish slavery. Because of their leadership, both became president. Washington was the first president of the

United States, and Lincoln was the sixteenth. Washington and Lincoln were two of this country's best leaders.

CONTRAST

Sometimes it is desirable to look at differences instead of similarities. A paragraph developed in this manner focuses only on ways in which the subjects are different. It does not treat similarities. Here is an example:

> A breakfast on a low-fat diet looks quite different from one in which fat is no consideration. Imagine this: fresh slices of pineapple and cantaloupe accompanied by crusty toasted bread with thin slices of Swiss cheese, some marmalade, and steaming black coffee. That's quite a switch from the traditional plate of fried ham and eggs, crisp hash browns, and hot biscuits with gravy, butter, and jam. Scores of middle-aged Americans have made the switch from high-fat to low, and they are finding that low-fat doesn't necessarily mean bad taste, little eye appeal, or low morale—just healthier hearts and happier bodies.

Donna Tobey points to even more differences in her delightful piece that contrasts Martha Stewart's approach to organization and her own:

> Ah! The joy of feeling organized! Thanksgiving weekend usually finds me with a day to myself and time to clean out a closet (or two), sort through old clothes, and reorganize dresser drawers before the onslaught of the December holidays. I did just that last week, and I was feeling pretty good about the job I had done, when I happened to catch a special program on television by Martha Stewart on . . . organizing one's clothes. The show began with Martha showing us how to wash sweaters. The first thing SHE does is draw a diagram of the sweater; then she measures the sweater with a tape measure, recording all dimensions on the diagram in order to "block" it properly when she removes it from the "ice cold" water and Woolite. I, on the other hand, throw the sweaters into one of those bags for dry-cleaning in a home dryer. After thirty minutes in the dryer, I toss the sweaters out of the bag, fold them, and put them away. Martha then showed us how she organizes her dresser drawers. She begins by taking the dimensions of the bottom of the drawers. Then she cuts heavy cardboard to fit the bottom. She glues *velvet* to the card-

board using special glue that will not attract moths, and, finally, she reloads the drawers with everything folded in very wonderful ways. My method it much easier—I reload the drawers with everything folded as best I can. Before the show ended, Martha let us know that these ideas, and MANY MORE, are in her current magazine. I just may pick up the issue. After all, I have lots of time for reading it because I am not measuring my sweaters to prepare them for "blocking" or waiting for glue to dry on my drawer liners.

Two more models come from Count Philippe Paul de Ségur's *Napoleon's Russian Campaign*. The first is from the section entitled "Napoleon Returns to Moscow":

The terrain he had to cross to reach Moscow presented a strange appearance. Enormous fires had been lit in the middle of the fields, in thick, cold mud, and were being fed with mahogany furniture and gilded windows and doors. Around these fires, on litters of damp straw, ill-protected by a few boards, soldiers and their officers, mud-stained and smoke-blackened, were seated in splendid armchairs or lying on silk sofas. At their feet were heaped or spread out cashmere shawls, the rarest of Siberian furs, cloth of gold from Persia, and silver dishes in which they were eating coarse black bread, baked in the ashes, and half-cooked, bloody horseflesh—strange combination of abundance and famine, wealth and filth, luxury and poverty! (p. 113)

The second is from the section, "From Kovno to Paris":

Here were the same valleys down which had poured those three long columns of dragoons and heavy cavalry, three streams of steel and brass, flashing in the hot sunlight. But now, men, weapons, eagles, horses, sunlight, even the frontier river they had crossed in such ardor and hope—everything had disappeared. The Niemen was just a long mass of blocks of ice piled up and welded together by the breath of winter. In place of the three French bridges brought fifteen hundred miles and erected with such daring speed, there was only one Russian bridge. Instead of the four hundred thousand companions who had fought so many successful battles with them, who had rushed so valiantly into Russia, they saw issuing from the white, ice-bound desert only one thousand foot soldiers and troopers still armed, nine cannon, and twenty thousand beings clothed in rags, with bowed heads, dull eyes, ashy, cadaverous faces, and long ice-stiffened beards. Some of them were fighting in silence for the right to cross the bridge which, despite their reduced number, was still too narrow to accommodate their precipitous flight. Others had rushed down the bank and were struggling across the river, crawling from one jagged cake of ice to another. And this was the Grand Army! (pp. 280–81)

Model Appropriate for the Early Grades

When Mama goes to town, she lets us stay with Grandmother. We like that. Mama lets us have only two cookies in the afternoon, but Grandmother lets us eat cookies until they're all gone. Also, Grandmother lets us play with her paints and canvas. Mama would never do that. But Mama lets us climb the tree, and Grandmother won't. So it's fun to have Mama home, and it's also fun to stay with Grandmother. They're just different.

Model Appropriate for the Middle Grades

Heavy objects can be moved with a lever or a pulley. A lever is a strong, rigid rod or stick, while a pulley is a wheel with a grooved rim with a rope going through it. A lever is put under the object to be moved, but a pulley is put over it, with the rope attached to the object, usually by a hook. To use a lever, you have to push down on the free end. To use a pulley, you have to pull on the rope.

COMPARISON AND CONTRAST

Discussing similarities and differences in the same essay challenges even the best writers. This strategy requires that the writer think and write about two subjects at once; further, the author must deal with both the similarities and the differences in the same passage. Here is an example:

Reading and writing are like ham and eggs. They go together, almost as one dish. There are differences, too, though, and those differences are important to teachers and students. Reading is a gathering skill; through it, we collect information, ideas, and images in our consciousness. And while writing is sometimes a gathering skill, when it helps us discover what we know or "collect our thoughts," it is primarily a sharing skill. We use it to share what we know with others. Both are active pastimes (the big word is *transactional*); they require our engagement. The kind of engagement, though, differs.

With reading, we are the receiver in the game, "receiving" text produced by someone else, whereas with writing, we're the quarterback, delivering text to the reader. The better we understand how these two skills are alike and how they are different, the better we can become at both. And skill in reading and writing opens the doors to academic success.

In the example above, the first sentence uses an analogy to introduce the two topics to be compared and contrasted. Then the passage develops similarities and differences. It concludes by connecting the similarities and differences and pointing out why understanding them is important. Following is another passage that uses the same organizational pattern.

Teaching and learning are two sides of the same fabric—not a right-side, wrong-side fabric but rather a reversible cloth, with both sides equally rich and beautiful. Teaching and learning are both essential to our growth as human beings. We grow by teaching—by being who we are and understanding that others will draw lessons from our beliefs and actions. We also grow by learning—by taking as our own the beliefs and actions what we admire in others. The role we play as teachers, though, differs from the role of learners. In usual circumstances, the teacher is more experienced, the learner less; the teacher more knowledgeable, the learner less; the teacher more confident, the learner less. Teaching and learning are both active pursuits. They differ in that teaching is the pursuit of giving and learning the pursuit of receiving. If we are truly whole, we are neither always one nor the other. Sometimes we are teachers and sometimes we are learners. In fact, sometimes we reverse roles. The father who teaches his daughter courage, confidence, and common sense may also learn from her curiosity, wonder, and sense of delight. The mother who teaches her son discipline, perseverance, and courage may also learn from him spontaneity, joy, and a sense of adventure. When we are successful at both teaching and learning, we double the beauty and value of our life's fabric.

Model Appropriate for the Early Grades

Apples and oranges are alike in some ways and different in others. Both are fruit. Both are round. Both are good to eat. But apples are red and oranges are orange. Apples are crisp, but oranges are soft. Apples have brown seeds, and oranges have white seeds.

Model Appropriate for the Middle Grades

The sisters looked so much alike that people who didn't know them tended to think they were twins. They were the same height and the same weight, and their coloring was similar: blonde hair, blue eyes, and fair complexion. They wore the same kinds of clothes, traditionally styled and well tailored. Those who knew them, though, realized that their personalities were poles apart. Shandra, the older, was outgoing, confident, and cheerful. Her little sister, Kendra, was shy, cautious, and quiet. Shandra was eager to step out and take risks, but Kendra always waited for someone else to go first. Their outward appearance belied their differences.

QUESTION-ANSWER

An effective technique for developing an idea is to ask a question and then answer it. Author Barry Lopez uses this device in his discussion of the narwhal in *Arctic Dreams: Imagination and Desire in a Northern Landscape*:

A remaining question is, Why is the tusk of the narwhal twisted? D'Arcy Wentworth Thompson, a renowned English biologist who died in 1948, offered a brilliant and cogent answer. He argued that the thrust of a narwhal's tail applied a very slight torque to its body. The tusk, suspended tightly but not rigidly in its socket in the upper jaw, resisted this force with a very slight degree of success. In effect, throughout its life, the narwhal revolved slowly around its own tusk, and over the years irregularities of the socket gouged the characteristic striations in the surface of the tooth. (p. 147)

The pattern Mr. Lopez uses is transition ("A remaining question is . . .") plus question ("Why is the tusk . . .?") plus author of answer ("D'Arcy Wentworth Thompson . . .") plus an identifying phrase that establishes credibility ("a renowned English biologist . . .") plus prediction of the answer ("offered a brilliant and cogent answer") plus answer ("He argued that . . .").

A paragraph modeled after Mr. Lopez's work might be the penultimate paragraph in an essay on Fitzroy Maclean's assessment of Tito shortly after he had parachuted into Yugoslavia to aid the then guerilla leader. (Maclean includes these facts about Tito in his fine book *Eastern Approaches*, an account of the author's activities just before and throughout World War II.)

The introduction of the essay would have established the subject of the essay as a discussion of Maclean's assessment of Tito's success as a guerilla leader and also McLean's qualifications for doing so (Maclean was a British general); it would also have predicted as subtopics (1) Tito's fervent commitment to communism, (2) his immense popularity with the common people of Yugoslavia, and (3) his flexibility and mobility as a military leader. Thus, the paragraph here would be the fourth in a five-paragraph essay, the first three having been the introduction and coverage of subtopics (1) and (2). Now, the model:

> A remaining question is, How was Tito able to garner victory after victory in the guerilla warfare in which he and his ill-equipped forces were immersed? McLean, known widely for his own military exploits in both Russia and North Africa, argues that Tito's military successes were the direct result of his flexibility and mobility. Tito was steadfast in his goals—defeating the invading Germans and establishing a communist government in Yugoslavia—but he was eminently pliant in his approach to achieving those goals. He sought opportunities to raid, deter, or demobilize the Germans, and finding his chances, he responded inventively and strategically, striking quickly and then moving on. He knew, too, that the moving on was essential for success. He never established a permanent headquarters, and he never sought to defend a position. Rather, he and his troops were elusive targets, striking in one place, then fading into the forests and hills to strike again on another day in a distant locale.

To help you analyze the process of modeling, look back at the two paragraphs, the one about narwhals and the one about Tito. How are they alike? How are they different?

A simpler form of the question-answer strategy is found in David Mitchell's essay "On Historical Fiction," in a reader's guide to *The Thousand Autumns of Jacob de Zoet*:

> Why, then, the enduring popularity of historical fiction? One reason is that it delivers a stereo narrative: from one speaker comes the treble of the novel's own plot while the other plays the bass of history's plot. A second reason is genealogical: if History is the family tree of Now, a historical novel (such as Alex Haley's *Roots*) may illuminate the contemporary world in ways that straight

history may not. The novel's ace of spades is subjective experience, which is a merit or demerit depending on how the card is played and who you are—Margaret Mitchell's *Gone with the Wind* can be either a sublime evocation or a toxic travesty. A third reason for the genre's popularity is simply that while the needs of the human heart and body stay much the same, the societies they must live in vary dramatically between centuries and cultures, and to watch people live—people whom we might have been had we been born then—under different regimes and rules is fascinating for its own sake. (pp. 487–88)

Mitchell asks his question by beginning with the key word *why*. He gives a three-part answer, introducing each part with simple transitions: *one reason, a second reason*, and *a third reason*. Far from being simplistic, though, his paragraph is rich with substantive ideas and figurative language.

Following is a paragraph that uses Mitchell's model. It could be part of a longer paper on a school's project to assess thinking and writing. Imagine that the preceding paragraph had praised the school's academic program.

Why, then, the need for a project to assess thinking and writing? One reason is that it amplifies the effort to provide a "rigorous education that incorporates all forms of critical thinking" promised by the school in its goals and criteria. Shining the spotlight on the school-wide project places it center stage, reinforcing the fact that thinking plays the leading role in the complex drama of an effective education. A second reason is practical: if teachers agree on what constitutes good thinking and writing, that agreement militates against grade inflation (or deflation) and standardizes high expectations across the curriculum, providing a strong, consistent framework for instruction throughout the school. A third reason for the project's need is simply the value of keeping score: assessing students' writing in a formal setting and reporting the results heighten awareness of strengths and gaps in students' learning, thus providing the basis for improvement in teaching.

Model Appropriate for the Early Grades

Why do we study music? We learn to sing because it's fun. We learn to play an instrument so we can entertain our friends and family and ourselves. It's also nice to know how to read music because then you can play and sing new songs. Finally, knowing music might get you a scholarship someday.

Model Appropriate for the Middle Grades

Why did Atticus Finch defend Tom Robinson in *To Kill a Mockingbird*? He knew that, in Maycomb County, a black man was not likely to be found innocent, no matter what the charges. But Atticus was an honorable man. He believed in Tom's innocence, and even more, he believed that Tom deserved a fair trial. By taking the case, he ensured that Tom would be defended as well as possible. He also knew that by defending Tom, he was setting an example for his children, Scout and Jem, teaching them that every human being has inalienable rights.

TRADITIONAL NARRATIVE

You know from having heard and read fairy tales and other children's stories the structure of a traditional narrative. (*Narrative* is another word for story.) The story opens with a phrase that denotes time (chronological means in order of time), such as "Once upon a time," "Long ago," "In the days of . . ." It continues by introducing early in the story, sometimes in the first sentence, a hero or heroine who will be on a quest, or adventure, to find something of value, to solve a problem, or to meet a challenge. The story depicts dangers or struggles, all of which are met and overcome by the hero or heroine. It ends with a satisfactory, and usually, happy resolution, with the leading characters living "happily ever after." This traditional narrative format can be used for children's stories or, as you will see from the following paragraphs, it can be used to tell adult stories as well.

Once upon a time in the land of Middle School, a splendid teacher named Allison Alpen decided that she would lead her students out of the land of illiteracy and into the Kingdom of Reading and Writing. Ms. Alpen was faced with challenges that would daunt the bravest dragon-slayer: resistant children, apathetic parents, too much television, too few books. But she persisted with her dream, and through the use of computers, artwork, magazines, music, books, compositions, and a great deal of HARD WORK, she guided her charges from the darkness into the light! Now her former students are successful in high school and their futures lie shining before them, for they live happily in the Kingdom of Reading and Writing.

Here is another paragraph that follows the same pattern:

Long ago in the town of Jamestown, New York, a baby girl was born. She grew up wanting to be an actress, but in the acting school she attended as a young woman, she was told that she would never be a success as an actress. She later said the only thing she learned in that school was how to be frightened. After that experience, she modeled a while, but a bout with rheumatic fever interfered and kept her from working at all for two years. Regaining her health, she worked as a cigarette girl, then as minor characters in radio drama. Still pursuing her dream, she moved to Hollywood, where she took on role after role in B movies—so many that she became known as "Queen of the Bs." Who would have known from those early years that the dedicated, persistent young woman would become one of the best-known and most popular actresses in the United States? Lucille Ball, the star of "I Love Lucy," "The Lucy-Desi Comedy Hour," "The Lucy Show," "Here's Lucy," and "Life with Lucy." She won four Emmys, the Women in Film Crystal Award, the Golden Globe Cecil B. DeMille Award, the Lifetime Achievement Award from the Kennedy Center, and the Governors Award from the Academy of Television Arts and Sciences. She went on to be the first woman to run a television studio, one that produced hits such as "Mission Impossible" and "Star Trek." After a most inauspicious beginning, the red-haired comedienne became an inspiration for generations of actresses to follow.

Model Appropriate for the Early Grades

Once upon a time in the Land of Dreams, a fairy princess was stolen from her castle by a wicked green monster. The monster kept the princess locked up in a cage. He fed her bread and water. She thought she would die there. But a handsome prince found out about her, and he came to her rescue. The prince waved a magic wand that made the monster turn good. The monster let the princess go. She married the prince, and they lived happily ever after.

Model Appropriate for the Middle Grades

Long ago in the Land of Lido, a wizard discovered that, by making a magic potion, he could turn ignorant children into brilliant people. He was about to use his potion on all of the children in the land when a villain named Roshmatoth stole the potion! Everyone searched high and low for Roshmatoth, but they couldn't find him anywhere. Then one day, three of the children were playing in a cave. There they discovered the hidden potion. Each took a sip. Voila! They turned into brilliant people. They put their new minds together, figured out where Roshmatoth was, captured him, and returned to the wizard triumphant. With the regained potion, the wizard turned all of the children into brilliant people, and they all lived happily ever after.

POINT-COUNTERPOINT

An appealing variation of the traditional paragraph structure of topic sentence followed by supporting details is the use of "point, counterpoint, development." This organization is found in Barry Lopez's description of the underwater sounds of the Arctic Ocean in his book *Arctic Dreams: Imagination and Desire in a Northern Landscape*. As you read, also note the effective use of fragments rather than complete sentences.

> The Arctic Ocean can seem utterly silent on a summer day to an observer standing far above. If you lowered a hydrophone, however, you would discover a sphere of "noise" that only spectrum analyzers and tape recorders could unravel. The tremolo moans of bearded seals. The electric crackling of shrimp. The baritone boom of walrus. The high-pitched bark and yelp of ringed seals. The clicks, pure tones, birdlike trills, and harmonics of belugas and narwhals. The elephantine trumpeting of bowhead whales. Added to these animal noises would be the sounds of shifting sediments on the sea floor, the whine and fracture of sea ice, and the sound of deep-keeled ice grounding in shallow water. (p. 147)

The pattern Mr. Lopez uses is point ("The Arctic Ocean can seem utterly silent) plus counterpoint ("If you lowered a hydrophone, however, you would discover . . .") plus development ('The tremolo . . . ice grounding in shallow water"). In this instance, development consists of six fragments and one concluding sentence.

The following paragraph uses the same pattern:

> Jamie Rickett's Advanced Placement English class appears to the untrained observer to be a freewheeling, intuitive discussion of some literary kernel. To the informed eye, however, it is clear that the class is an artful orchestration

of academic inquiry by a master teacher. The tennis-serve gesture that lobs probing questions into the midst of furrowed brows. The wide-eyed, quizzical expression coupled with rising inflection that challenges pat answers. The enforced silence after a question to allow students time to think. The beckoning gesture that invites elaboration of a promising response. The constant movement from the front to the center to the back to the sides of the room, reaffirming the ubiquitous nature of the teacher's voice. The smiles, groans, laughter that accompany students' odyssey into literary analysis. Underlying this mastery of technique is a wisdom borne of a cornucopian knowledge of literature and an abiding faith in the process of learning through inquiry.

Model Appropriate for the Early Grades

This strategy is not recommended for the early grades.

Model Appropriate for the Middle Grades

A highly skilled basketball team makes winning look easy. However, what you can't see when you watch those swift passes, perfect screens, seamless teamwork, and flawless shots are the hours and hours of practice that the players endured before game time. Drill after drill of dribbling and passing. Hundreds of free throws. Hours of handing off and laying up. Miles of running. Thousands of pushups. An equal number of pullups. The game's performance is like the tip of an iceberg; the bulk of it, all that practice beforehand that makes winning possible, is out of sight.

EXTENDED ANALOGY

An *analogy*, according to Webster's, is "a partial similarity between like features of two things, on which a comparison may be based: the *analogy between the heart and a pump*." A traditionally structured paragraph begins with a topic sentence that tells what the paragraph is going to be about and what the author is going to say about the topic. That sentence is followed by details that develop the idea stated in the topic sentence. A traditionally structured paragraph often ends with a concluding statement that sums up the paragraph. Combining an analogy with traditional paragraph structure results in a paragraph that describes one thing by comparing it to another. Here is a paragraph, for example, that compares animal and plant cells to a shoe factory. It was written by Heather Gillingham-Rivas.

results in a paragraph that describes one thing by comparing it to another. Here is a paragraph, for example, that compares animal and plant cells to a shoe factory. It was written by Heather Gillingham-Rivas.

> Animal and plant cells and their many organelles are like a shoe factory. Inside every factory can be found the office of the operations manager containing the secured files, paper or digital, for all operations, including the secret instructions for the most fashionable and comfortable shoes possible. In a cell, all instructions for the processes of that specific cell can be found in the nucleus, a structure enclosed by a membrane that contains the genetic information that, when read and converted into a useable format, can create any part of the cell and organism to which it belongs. Instructions to employees need to be delivered to them through the corridors of the building. In cells, the endoplasmic reticulum serves as hallways to move information from the nucleus to other parts of the cell. No factory can run without electricity, and likewise, a cell has organelles that function as a power plant. The mitochondria of cells take in raw materials to turn into chemical energy used all around the cell. In the Golgi apparatus and lysosome can be found the shoebox department and cleanup system for the factory. Plant and animal cells are very much like mini-shoe factories in the organisms in which they live.

Here is another example, written by Jeanne Sanford, entitled "The American Colonies: 'Child' of Great Britain."

> The relationship of the American colonies to Great Britain was very much like the relationship of a child to its mother. A mother nurtures a child from birth through childhood, providing the essential food, clothing, shelter, and protection in order to survive. Similarly, Great Britain, through private corporations as well as the Crown, sponsored settlements or colonies and provided manufactured goods and building materials which allowed the colonies to grow. In addition, the forts built by the British protected these colonies from both the French and the Indians. Over time, the colonies built cities and prosperous shipping ports, established churches, schools and universities, and local governments, not unlike the teenager who wants to create and explore the larger world. As the colonies grew and prospered, they began to wonder, "Are we British or American? Do we want Great Britain controlling our lives forever or do we want to become our own country, with our own identity and destiny?" The answer was, not unlike that of any older teenager, embarking on a new and exciting life, one in which the colonies hoped to

prosper and find their place in the world. The answer, of course, was independence, and it resulted in the creation of the Declaration of Independence, followed by the American Revolution.

Model Appropriate for the Early Grades

This strategy is not recommended for the early grades.

Model Appropriate for the Middle Grades

Friendship is like a bubble bath. When you first find a friend, both of you are excited and bubbling over with conversation. When you first get into a bubble bath, the water is warm and bubbles are everywhere. To keep the bubbles going and the water comfortable, though, you have to keep adding warm water. To keep a friendship going, you have to work at it, too. Otherwise, it will be like an untended bubble bath. It will grow lukewarm, then cold, and you will want to get out of it.

APPENDIX A
TEACHING THE ORGANIZATIONAL STRATEGIES

Teaching the Organizational Strategies

The Pattern	What It Does	When To Teach It	Good Prewriting Strategies	Sample Transitional Words	Sample Writing Tasks That Use It
Chronological	Presents details in the order in which they occurred	Pre-K on	Jot-listing, timelines	First, second, etc.; next, then, finally	Think about a time when you were really frightened. Tell your readers about it, in the order that it happened.
					Think about a time when you were really happy. Describe that time in detail for your readers, starting at the beginning.
Spatial	Organizes information according to space, or place	2nd grade on	Maps, diagrams	North, south, east, west Above, below To the right, to the left	Describe one of the rooms in your house, telling your readers about what they would see, one section at a time.
					Tell your readers how to get from school to your home. Describe landmarks that will guide them in their journey.
Topical	Organizes a broad subject by sub-topics, sometimes presenting in order of importance (most to least or least to most)	Pre-K on	Clustering, jot-listing, diagramming	Also, in addition, most important, least important	Tell your readers about something you really enjoy doing, giving three reasons why you like that activity.
					Describe your favorite holiday, telling about the three things you most enjoy about it.

Type	Description	Grade	Graphic Organizer	Transition Words	Assignment
Comparison	Shows similarities, or likenesses, of two or more subjects	3rd grade on	Parallel lists or boxes, clusters that link the likenesses	Similarly, likewise, just as..., and	Tell about the things that are alike in two of your best friends.
Contrast	Shows differences of two or more subjects	3rd grade on	Parallel lists or boxes, clusters that link the differences	On the other hand, but, however, on the contrary	Tell about the things that are alike in two of your favorite stories. Tell about the things that are different in two of your best friends.
Comparison and Contrast	Shows both similarities and differences of subjects	4th grade on	Venn Diagram	(See the words for comparison and contrast above)	Tell about the things that are different in two of your favorite stories. Combine the two pieces about your best friends into one essay. Combine the two pieces about your favorite stories into one essay.
Question-Answer	Asks a question and then answers it	3rd grade on	Jot-listing, talking through possible answers	Depends upon how the answer is developed	Ask a question about a subject you know well. Then answer the question fully, with examples and elaboration.
Traditional Narrative	Tells a story with beginning, middle, and end	3rd grade on	Oral telling of the story, informal or formal outline	Those suitable for chronological organization (see above)	Make up a story with a hero or heroine who faces a problem; tell how the problem is resolved and then end the story.
Point-Counterpoint	Begins with an assertion, continues with statement that contradicts assertion, and develops the contradiction	6th grade on	Discussion	However, on the contrary, but (between assertion and contradiction)	State a misconception some grown-ups have about teenagers. Then state what is actually true. Develop the statement about what is actually true with details from your own and your friends' experiences.
Extended Analogy	Compares something to another thing that is usually not considered similar	6th grade on	Maps, clusters, diagrams	Similarly, likewise, also	Tell how the heart is like a pump, how friendship is like a garden, or how the brain is like a computer.

APPENDIX B
SEAGRASS AND SILVER: A LESSON IN MODELING RHYTHM AND RHYME

EXPLANATION OF THE LESSON

Sometime you might want to lead your students through the delightful experience of modeling rhythm and rhyme. Here is one way to do it. Although this lesson was originally conceived for senior high school students, it could be modified for any age by choosing appropriate rhyme and rhythm and by eliminating the technical vocabulary if it's too advanced for your students.

PURPOSES OF THE LESSON

The purposes of this lesson are to increase students' joy in language, their appreciation of the craft of poetry, and their engagement in learning.

LEARNING OBJECTIVES

After completing the lesson and the accompanying activities, students will be able to discern the rhythm and rhyme in a poem and model them in a work of their own.

MATERIALS NEEDED

- A poem suitable for the age and grade you teach, one copy without the meter marked and one with it marked.
- Optional but highly desirable, a poem that models the rhythm.
- Examples of the rhythm you're teaching.
- A whiteboard, Smartboard, PowerPoint, or some other platform for showing the examples that illustrate the meter.
- A worksheet with the rhythm marked and with lines for students to create their own poem.

DIRECTIONS

Share Sara Teasdale's poem, "I Would Live in Your Love" (it follows), by reading it aloud several times to show students how the undulation of the waves is manifest in the rhythm of the poem (anapestic pentameter in the first and third lines, anapestic hexameter in the second and fourth lines). (An *anapest* is a foot with two unstressed syllables followed by one stressed. *Pentameter* indicates a line with five [*penta*] feet [*meter*] and *hexameter* a line with six [*hexa*] feet [*meter*].)

Then show students how to scan the poem and mark the anapestic feet. (The second copy that follows is marked for you.) You might point out that anapestic rhythm also reflects well the rhythm of galloping horses, and illustrate that point by reading aloud a few lines of anapestic tetrameter (four anapestic feet per line, tetra meaning four) from Byron's "The Destruction of Sennacherib": "The Assyrian came down like a wolf on the fold! And his cohorts were gleaming in purple and gold."

Next, mark on the board one line of stressed and unstressed symbols that designate anapestic pentameter (the small *u* represents unstressed and the / stressed):

u u / u u / u u / u u / u u /

and one that depicts anapestic hexameter:

u u / u u / u u / u u / u u / u u /

Let students play with sounds and words that create lines that have the designated rhythm. Examples of anapestic pentamenter:

How I love to go swimming in Sweetwater Creek in the spring!
Did you know that Sue Johnson was older than Becky or me?
He did not tell a lie, but he certainly garbled the truth.

Examples of anapestic hexameter:

Don't you think that the children sing louder than all of the rest of the
   group?
Give me salad and pasta and garlic, with crusty French bread on the side.
Sing along with the angels in heav'n as rejoicing and song fill the air.

Write the lines on the board. Scan them to prove their meter. This part of the lesson should not be rushed (or any of it, for that matter). Students need to discern that words may span feet, that words out of the context of a line of poetry may have a different rhythm from the same words within the context of a scanned line, and that words can be rearranged to produce the idea and rhythm desired.

Finally, give students a sheet with the stressed and unstressed syllables marked for each line, modeled after Teasdale's poem. Ask them to create a four-line poem that has the same or nearly the same rhythm as the original. Students' poems may rhyme, or not, as the authors choose. You may wish to point out that the rhyme scheme of the original poem is abab.

Following are Teasdale's poem; the same poem with foot, meter, and rhyme marked; a poem that models the rhythm of Teasdale's poem, but not exactly (all of the lines are anapestic pentameter); and the worksheet you may use for your students to model Teasdale's poem.

I Would Live in Your Love
by Sara Teasdale
I would live in your love as the seagrasses live in the sea,
Borne up by each wave as it passes, drawn down by each wave that recedes.
I would empty my soul of the dreams that are gathered in me,
I would beat with your heart as it beats, I would follow your soul as it leads.

I Would Live in Your Love
by Sara Teasdale

```
u  u   /   u  u   /   u  u /   u   u /   u u  /

I would live| in your love| as the sea|grasses live| in the sea,|

u   u  /   u   u   /     u u /    u   u   /    u u   /

Borne up | by each wave | as it pass | es, drawn down | by each wave |

    u  u  /

    that recedes.|

u   u   /    u  u /   u u  /      u  u   /   u   u /

I would emp | ty my soul | of the dreams | that are ga | thered in me,|

u   u   /    u   u   /    u u /    u  u   /   u u   /

I would beat | with your heart | as it beats, | I would fol | low your soul |

    u  u  /

    as it leads.|
```

(Note that *borne* is read slowly, to take the "space" of two unstressed syllables.)

Silver
by Billie Birnie
Silver sky, silver sails, silver fish, silver bird, silver sand,
Why is silver at sea so much better than gold on the land?
It responds to the rhythm of waves and the changes of sun,
It reflects all the beauty men fail to perceive as they run.

WORK SHEET FOR MODELING THE RHYTHM OF "I WOULD LIVE IN YOUR LOVE"

u   u /   u   u   /   u   u   /   u   u   /   u   u   /
_____

u u /   u   u   /   u   u   /   u   u   /   u   u   /   u   u   /
_____

u   u /   u   u   /   u   u   /   u   u   /   u   u   /
_____

u u /   u   u   /   u   u   /   u   u   /   u   u   /   u   u   /
_____

REFERENCES

Claggett, Fran, et al. 2005. *Teaching Writing: Craft, Art, Genre*. Urbana, IL: National Council of Teachers of English.

De Ségur, Count Philippe Paul. 1958. *Napoleon's Russian Campaign*. New York: Time.

Gallagher, Kelly. 2011. *Write Like This: Teaching Real-World Writing Through Modeling and Mentor Texts*. Portland, ME: Stenhouse.

Gwynne, S. C. 2010. *Empire of the Summer Moon*. New York: Scribner.

Lopez, Barry. 1986. *Arctic Dreams: Imagination and Desire in a Northern Landscape*. Toronto: Bantam Books.

Maclean, Fitzroy. 2004. *Eastern Approaches*. New York: Penguin Global.

Mitchell, David. 2011. *The Thousand Autumns of Jacob de Zoet*. New York: Random House.

O'Brian, Patrick. 1983. *Treason's Harbour*. New York: W. W. Norton.

Silverstein, Shel. 1974. *Where the Sidewalk Ends: The Poems and Drawings of Shel Silverstein*. New York: HarperCollins.

Strunk, William, Jr., and E. B. White. 2005. *The Elements of Style*. New York: Penguin Press.

Teasdale, Sara. 1911. *Helen of Troy and Other Poems by Sara Teasdale*. New York: Original publisher unknown. Available online through Project Gutenberg.

Tufte, Virginia. 2006. *Artful Sentences: Syntax as Style*. Cheshire, CT: Graphics Press.

ABOUT THE AUTHOR

Billie F. Birnie has been teaching writing most of her life, first to students in elementary, middle, and senior high schools, and, in recent years, to prospective and experienced teachers. Her published writing ranges from poetry and memoir to professional articles and books on teaching and learning. A charter staff member of the Glazer-Lorton Writing Institute in Miami, Florida, Dr. Birnie has received numerous awards for her work in education: she was named Teacher of the Year in two large urban high schools, Distinguished Alumnus by the University of Miami School of Education, and Educator of the Year by Florida International University. She can be contacted at bfbirnie@bigbend.net.